JOEL HILAIRE, M.D.

The
SILENT
SONG

AuthorHouse™
1663 Liberty Drive
Bloomington, IN 47403
www.authorhouse.com
Phone: 1 (800) 839-8640

Published by AuthorHouse 04/05/2018

ISBN: 978-1-5462-3591-0 (sc)
ISBN: 978-1-5462-3592-7 (e)

Library of Congress Control Number: 2018903920

Print information available on the last page.

Any people depicted in stock imagery provided by Getty Images are models,
and such images are being used for illustrative purposes only.
Certain stock imagery © Getty Images.

This book is printed on acid-free paper.

Because of the dynamic nature of the Internet, any web addresses or links contained in this book may have changed
since publication and may no longer be valid. The views expressed in this work are solely those of the author and do not
necessarily reflect the views of the publisher, and the publisher hereby disclaims any responsibility for them.

authorHOUSE®

CONTENTS

FOREWORD

One can say so much when in reality nothing was said. We have been told that a portrait can transpire a thousand words. In these same thought processes, I can say that The Silent Song goes far beyond the melodies of music in tone, messages, and emotions. It is a gallery of different portraits in verse, by one painter (the poet), who has skillfully learned to blend different hues of color.

This collection of poems takes one on a spiritual journey that expresses love in its finest form. It also provides the reality of responsibility for one who has "been selected" to lead a church. This is done in an enlightening manner with teachings. Who would think that you could learn about biblical characters, their attributes, and even family history, by reading poems? Yet, this is what the author does, and it captures one's undivided attention from start to finish.

It doesn't stop there however... There are also portraits in verse in this collection of poems that express pain and suffering. The message to grasp is clear: understanding how to effectively deal with our darker days by singing The Silent Song. Sometimes it is not only through prayer that the heavenly Father can answer, but He does also through silence. This hearing can allow us to see past our differences, our own will, and our own desires to live a life dedicated to righteousness. Not only so, but to also know that there is comfort that can be transpired by words, music, tears and art, and many more to say the least. With The Silent Song, one can walk through a well captured journey that begins and ends through the beautiful art gallery of life.

From one poet to another, I would like to conclude with this refrain of mine:

THE ART OF SILENCE

❖

Silence is the art,
That I am learning to paint on the canvas of my heart.

It shades downward in its humbleness
To allow the colors to brighten like a furnace.

The colorful pinwheel studies to be quiet
While it contemplates the texture
God freelanced will is creating.

It glazes immensely in prayer
While the mirage begins to reflect its maker.

The resin of submission is mysterious,
As it allows me to love to the next upward stroke of God's brush.

There's so much more for silence to paint,
As I mature into God's sufficient grace.

Magdaline Filsaime

PREFACE

❧

Silence does not mean ignorance like meekness is not synonymous of weakness. Silence is not a result of fear or a sign of cowardice. In fact, it takes courage and strength to remain poise and silent when facing adversity in life. "He that has knowledge spares his words ..." said a wise man, "...and he who rules his spirit is better than he who takes a city." An author even admonished us "to study to be quiet"! Jesus did just that when his accusers dragged him whether before the council, or Pilate, or before Herod the king. There are times in life where keeping silent is the wisest attitude one can adopt.

This is the lesson one can find in The Silent Song. This book can be seen as a complement to what has started in the author's recently published poetry book, Gemstone. The Silent Song takes the reader to a higher level of spirituality where one learns to remain poise as he controls the turmoil of his inner world.

The Silent Song displays a collection of poems where the author is showing another step, another level in his quest toward reaching spiritual growth and maturity. One's life always speaks louder than just his words. A silent preacher living a righteous and holy life can say more by his actions than an eloquent one that relies mainly on his words to influence people around him. Someone once said, "I'd rather see a sermon than hear one."

May The Silent Song be an inspiration to you all.

THE SELECTED ONE

❧

Listen, I have been selected
To be where you see me today.
It's not what I always wanted,
But now it's clearly my pathway.

It is scary to see beyond
And quite also astonishing
To be able to hear beyond …
Could be a curse or a blessing!

See beyond looks in the future
To what others cannot conceive;
Hear beyond catches the murmur
That nobody else has perceived.

In either case it's not easy
To blurt out in the open
What seems to be a big mystery
To those whose hearts life has hardened.

Listen, I have been selected.
To walk this way, I have no choice.
I talk when others stay quiet,
Withdraw when others lift their voice.

I have to keep my eyes open
When others feel tired and rest.
My sword has to be well sharpened
When on my way come all the tests.

No matter what others may do,
No matter what others may think,
I just can't say, "I'll follow too."
For I cannot let my ship sink.

Lord, please, my shoulder piece, strengthen
So I can carry my burdens.
Like you, I have been selected.
Let me firmly walk till the end.

⚜

THE CHOSEN ONE

To Ramona!

❧

You have been called the Chosen One
Really for specific reasons,
And this is not a light matter
For someone with your character.

In you dwells your father's spirit,
A deep source of inspiration,
To help you change people's habits
With constant care and compassion.

Challenges lie on your pathway
And, at times, within your own self.
Overcoming them every day
Can fill you with peace and good health.

Your intuition and your insight,
As sharp and strong as your knowledge,
Can be a bright light in the night
To those who could feel discouraged.

The Chosen One, you have been called,
To clearly make a difference.
You may well say nothing at all;
Yet tell so much by your presence.

Your gift makes you so powerful,
And yet you know that your best tool
Is none but your humility,
Coupled with some simplicity.

The Chosen One: a fine fabric
You carry with such elegance!
Honoring your father's ethics,
It's how you will make a difference.

———————❧———————

THE DREAM

To my wife, Claire!

❧

My dove, my only dove!
You shower me with love,
So much now every day,
My mind is blown away.

Your heartbeats seem to sing
The purest melodies
That one can only bring
From (the) land of symphonies.

Your kind smile is a light
Shining into my world,
Sending waves of delight
That make me want to twirl.

You seem to be a dream:
The best I've ever had.
Out of joy I could scream
To show I am that glad!

But I don't want to break
The spell of that sweet love
That fits me like a glove
And causes me to shake.

Love is such a mystery.
You risk great misery
When in innocency,
You break its secrecy.

So awaken me not
While I am tenderly
At last tying a knot
With so sweet memories!

I am that honeybee
Flying over your heart,
Looking for a soft part
To produce pure honey.

You are that field of dreams
I get now to explore;
You are my special realm
Where I hide to adore.

I am that singing bird,
Flying over your head,
With tender melodies
You call your remedies.

You're my refreshing lake
In which I love to swim
To get rid of the aches
That used to make me scream.

You are my eyes' delight;
Yet my hidden weapon;
Whether to fly or fight,
You're my inspiration.

You are, you are, you are
All that I can't express.
I know by now, my dove,
Words can become senseless
When one has found access
To the pathway of love.

———————— ❧ ————————

THE UGLY FACE OF SIN

❧

The king was bored in his palace
As away for war went his hosts.
Not used to stay still in one place,
He felt so useless and so lost.

He sought refuge from his boredom
On the royal house rooftop,
Not knowing there, in his kingdom,
He would suffer a shameful drop.

In the beauty of the evening,
He found an evening of beauty:
A woman herself was washing,
Exposing her tempting body.

Bath-Sheba, he learned, was her name:
Eliam's daughter, Uriah's wife.
Yet he was burning in such flame
He no longer cared for his life!

If Ahithophel he had called,
His counselor and trusted friend,
He could have been saved from that fall
And remained sole king of the land.

Ahithophel, Eliam's father,
Would know well what to David say
To prevent the dreadful letter
That claimed Uriah's life away.

But to do so King David failed.
He kissed the ugly face of sin
Discovered right behind the veil
Of the passion under his skin.

A wife lost her integrity,
While her dear husband lost his life;
A child lived a short destiny.
A good friend was caught in a strife,

Before committing suicide
In a shocking and vain attempt
His loved ones' dishonor to hide
And to bury his own contempt.

The king did regret his mistake,
But to erase it was too late
For life allows only one take
To set and to define one's fate.

Remember that one always pays
For every deed along the way.
Whatever he does or he says
Will surely affect his pathway.

———————❧———————

EZEKIEL

❧

He was called both priest and prophet.
Jeremiah, Zechariah:
Chosen ones to share the same fate,
They all abode by the Torah.

When exploring Ezekiel's life,
To see it can be disturbing
That his own will, wellness, or wife
At one point carried no meaning.

To be chosen as man of God
Is abdicating one's own right;
You learn to uphold high his Word
And let around shine his bright light.

A little book he had to eat,
Sweet in the mouth as pure honey,
But when came time out to spit,
It was bitter in the belly.

No matter how others may feel,
The message from the little book
Completely ought to be fulfilled
In those who, to serve him, look.

The man of God always is used
To awaken the people's minds
On what the Lord wants them to choose
Or on new thoughts for them to find.

Why should he eat a special cake
With such specific ingredients?
Why should he use cow's dung to bake
What will become his regimen?

Why when it's time for him to sleep
He can't even relax in bed?
His comfort setting he must skip
While people's sins on him were laid.

He may have suffered many things
While with the book content dealing,
Yet couldn't he fathom the saying
That came to him that sad morning:

"Son of man, see, I'll take away
Your eyes' delight, your heart's passion.
With a stroke she will go today
And leave you with no companion.

Yet you can't cry or a tear shed.
You cannot mourn and cannot weep.
Just bind the tire of your head
While you cannot cover your lips."

Ezekiel spoke in the morning.
Without any transition,
His dear wife died in the evening.
He had to hide his emotions.

Where, o Lord, did he find the strength
To endure such calamities?
Can one go through all that at length
Yet survive those adversities?

When God to serve Him calls a man,
He takes the time to equip him.
As Ezekiel means "God strengthens,"
His sense of pain God must have dimmed.

How one today sees Ezekiel
His dedication will affect;
And to be that wheel in the wheel
Wants one to have no more defects.

———————❧———————

THE SILENT SONG

The art of silence I'm learning
To bring to my heart and my mind
A brand-new melody to sing,
And a new way to become kind.

I need to tune out the noise
All around me that is raging;
I am developing the poise
That comes only from clean living.

A lake so peaceful and serene
Surrounded by tall and green trees
Is now the new scenery I see
As my eyes I close to my pain.

A sure refuge this has become
When to connect with me I need.
I discover there a sweet balm
To soothe my heart, my soul to feed.

The art of silence I'm learning
To strengthen my inner being;
I love the peace I feel within
Since now this silent song I sing.

———— ❧ ————

TELL ME

❧

Tell me! Tell me that it's a dream
That will go away very soon
So I have no reason to scream
And behave like an old baboon.

Tell me I am not hitting a wall
While I am trying to reason
And addressing a simple call
To bring a sense of cohesion.

Everything around us can change
In just a twinkling of an eye;
But we can always rearrange
What seems to be in disarray.

Nature teaches us great wisdom
As come and go all the seasons.
Nothing just happens at random
A skillful hand has all fashioned.

So learn to remain in silence
When it is hard to understand.
Simply because of your patience,
A new hope before you can stand.

SILENT PAIN

❧

As the lamb brought to the slaughter,
Knowing what's ahead to suffer
Yet moving with a steady pace,
I don't intend to leave this race.

At times I think I can no more,
But thanks to the God I adore,
I cannot really lose my hope
As he teaches me how to cope.

It does not matter how lonely,
Dark, scary, rainy, or slippery
The road to follow may appear.
All will be well with Jesus near.

I know that blood I haven't sweat.
Though my test is not complete yet,
I am learning through silent pain
To focus on the crown to gain.

❧

ALTAR TALK

❧

I come to your altar of grace
To pour my heart out to you;
I know there is no other place
Where I can find any solace.

Why should I let the storms of life
Affect the trust I have in you
Though as a deep cut of a knife,
I feel a sharp pain going through?

You have always been my fortress,
My sure refuge, my hiding place.
In you, I know, I can find rest
As I commit to your embrace.

So hear what I am not saying
As the words are running away.
You know what my heart is sighing
As I follow this steep pathway.

❧

REFLECTIONS

❧

Time can be a wall, a thick wall
Standing strong between two nations,
Two people, or generations
Who wish that didn't exist at all!

Distance can also be a wedge
Able to set people apart,
And yet can't remove from their heart
What to each other they have pledged.

Prejudice is a thick blinder
Which can rob us from life's beauty,
Keeping us in obscurity
While there's so much to discover!

Earth would be such a better place
If there were no segregation,
Abuse and discrimination
Among what is the human race.

Dishonoring diversity,
We create creed, color and race.
We've lost humility and grace
To embrace animosity.

What if we stop being selfish
To become each other's keepers?
What if we stop being haters
And learn our lives to embellish?

We were not placed here to destroy,
But to dress, to keep and maintain
What should have been our Eden
Created for us to enjoy.

We have all lost the clear vision
That was designed our steps to guide,
And teach us how well to abide
In a clean and holy nation.

Lord, help us to regain conscience
And find back the right direction;
We will end up in destruction
If we dwell in our ignorance.

❧

BOUNDARIES

❧

Understand: one can't always lean
Toward whatever comes his way.
All his steps he must maintain clean
As from the goal he does not sway.

There's a limit in everything.
And for every territory
One day he may be exploring,
He finds some lines called boundaries.

Nature at times displays pictures
On how vital boundaries are.
If our actions we don't censure,
We end up with terrible scars.

The earth despite its great beauty
When it's shaken by an earthquake
Becomes just rubbish and debris
Which are so difficult to rake.

The vast, blue, and poetic sea
Can quickly swirl and be wicked,
Producing a mean tsunami
Leaving behind so many dead!

The wind today, source of delight,
Can strengthen in a hurricane,
Filling the hearts with so much fright
That some of us become insane.

I like to know the earth won't slide,
Or the sea won't pass the seashore,
Or warm and cold airs won't collide
To trouble our inner core.

Boundaries in relationships
Are vital landmarks for safety.
We become as wandering ships
When we skip that reality.

Friendship and love are beautiful
When one maintains them clean and neat.
They can be a place so peaceful
That protects from life's storms and heat.

❧

THE SHADOW OF YOUR WINGS

❧

Under the shadow of your wings,
I long to find a sure refuge.
Under the shadow of your wings,
Protect me from this life's deluge.

Who else but you in all wisdom
Know how well to direct my steps?
How could I fit in your kingdom
If to me you did not send help?

I daily face mortality,
I fight against iniquity
While I dream of your Deity
Glowing with immortality.

You pull me from the miry clay,
Because for me you had a plan.
Why in this vile mud would I stay
When in your presence I could stand?

Strengthen me, o my precious Lord,
For a successful walk with you!
Teach me to use with skills your sword.
Show how nigh I can draw to you.

I know by now exists a life
More excellent than this one here,
Where no longer one faces strife
Pain, sorrow, fear, or bursts of tear.

I know for us all you provide
Divine manna, living water.
You're showing us how to abide
In your principles and order.

So your scroll, Lord, I eat slowly:
The taste in the mouth is so sweet!
I long to be just and holy.
Grant me to stay safe at your feet.

THE ROCK

❧

Let me lean on the mighty Rock,
The solid Rock of the ages,
As one from the Lord's blessed flock,
When around me the world rages.

It was there in the wilderness
For the Children of Israel.
And when they were facing distress,
To rescue them it never failed.

It is present for us today
To lend some help in any need.
It can well guide us day by day
If we just yield and let him lead.

The Rock can supply with water,
Living water quenching one's thirst,
Changing in righteous the sinner,
Teaching in life to put God first.

The Rock also can give honey:
For the heart, source of great delight,
Blessings that can buy no money,
Set for those that are walking right.

Out of the flinty Rock as well
Flows the oil of understanding.
One can learn how to safely dwell
In the land of the Mighty King.

Fire can proceed from the Rock
To purify or to consume,
Cleansing and purging from the flock
Whatever needs to go in fume.

Let me lean on the mighty Rock
Where is stored everything I need.
As a part of God's blessed flock,
In green pastures, I know, He'll lead.

❧

THE JOURNEY

❧

Everyone is in a journey
Since the day of birth till one dies.
Toward Destiny day by day
One must cope with what ahead lies.

Some have learned to travel real light.
Others carry heavy luggage.
Some can find in life true delight
Others mainly deal with damage.

Some, with what life hands them, do well.
Others hunt for ways of escape.
How to all others can one tell
How to embellish their landscape,

When as a sad, wandering soul
He errs around with so much lust
Instead of using his good tools
To inspire true love and trust?

How will one ever reach the goal
When one despises the landmarks
Set wisely to prevent his fall
And pull him away from the dark?

As pilgrim here and as stranger,
Why does one entangle himself
With what can get him endanger
And by sin get trapped and engulfed?

The seriousness of this journey
One can't continue to ignore.
It involves without delay
Deep changes in one's inner core.

Basic and advanced instructions
Are provided along the way
To prepare one for perfection
And free him from this house of clay.

One day all fight will be over.
One will reach the end of the road.
To carry there'll be no more load
Peace and joy will be forever.

❧

THE NEW SONG

❧

Since Jesus upon this earth came,
He opened the way to heaven.
He filled our hearts with a new flame
And great hope for a safe haven.

Since Jesus came into my heart,
Life for me took a new meaning.
He handed me a brand-new chart
Where I found a new song to sing.

The song of Moses and the Lamb
Isn't for anybody to learn.
It's not a song that you can cram.
The right to sing it you must earn.

This great song comes line upon line,
Also precept upon precept.
It is well tried and so refined.
You ought to learn it with respect.

Jesus came as the truth, the way,
And started to show how to sing.
He led men to a new pathway
To facilitate their learning.

Many to follow him refused
For men do not love humbleness.
But if his ways we learn to use,
We can discover true greatness.

Into my heart Jesus has come,
Showed me my need for the Father.
I know what my life can become.
So with my God I can gather.

A TIME TO GRIEVE

To Claire, after Sebastien's death

❦

She'll never be the same again
Since from us her son walked away.
He may no longer now feel pain
But she does not see it that way.

"My son, my son" she loved to say
As she patted him in the chest.
But she often now looked away
As she's left with an empty nest.

She was not ready - not so soon,
To let him travel all alone
When at least for another moon
She would enjoy him as her own.

Now to the land of memories
He belongs ... She can no longer,
When sitting by the computer,
Share with him family stories

Which would trigger fun and laughter
That only they both could enjoy,
As little children would their toys.

No more having those arguments
That seemed to create some frictions:
Others would be odd elements
In trying to bring solutions.

For the first time in four decades,
He will no longer be around.
How can we enjoy life's parade,
When the best drummer has left town?

He walked toward eternity,
The afterlife, that other place.
Some then lost their ability
To hug or to warmly embrace.

He could look simple as a child
Yet bigger than life he has been.
His dancing at times could get wild
Yet he managed to remain clean.

Life around suddenly can change
Bringing then some new beginning,
Beginning at times very strange
If one misses life's true meaning.

We'll never be the same again
As we're humming a silent song.
Whether in our heart or our brain
It seems that something has gone wrong.

Yet, regardless, we still believe
That someone cares for how we feel.
And as we're learning how to grieve
We hope one day we will be healed.

❧

BE STILL: KNOW THAT I AM GOD!

On the historic hurricane Irma of 08-09/2017

❧

Irma! Irma! What made you think
That coming way from Africa
You could force all of us to drink
From your cup of anathema?

Didn't you know that there is a God
Full of compassion and goodness
That covers by His precious blood
All those that seek in Him their rest?

To Saint Martin and Antigua
You have been truly merciless
As well to Cuba, Barbuda,
Porto-Rico and all the rest.

The list is long, you know it well.
You were ready to smash them all,
Forgetting that there is a bell
Held by the Master of us all.

Whenever to ring it He sets
No matter strong you think you are,
You have no choice but to reset
And, to obey Him, be prepared.

That is why when Haiti you reached,
The Voice came to you loud and clear:
"My Children, here, you cannot touch.
They have for too long lived in fear.

I desire them all to feel
How special to my heart they are!
In order for them to be healed
Of this great wrath they should be spared.

Irma quickly had to obey:
Over the sea she found her way,
Thinking that she would not be swayed
When she'll reached the Florida Keys!

She muscled up, thought Florida
Would be a second Barbuda.
Then from one coast to the other
She was ready all to cover.

In her mission of destruction
She already designed her way
And started well in full motion
Until the Master voiced His say:

"I have throughout all this land
Righteous Children at my service.
They must know with them strong I stand.
Their faith is not vain sacrifice."

Irma again didn't have a choice
And from a five became a two!
All it took was the Master's voice
To confuse the scientists too.

God was standing behind the scenes
To listen to His Children's cry,
To spare them from the things obscene
Ready to make them easy prey.

The testimonies now abound
On how God's hands had intervened.
You simply have to walk around
To hear the tales concerning Him!

To the Almighty be glory,
Honor and praise and majesty!
To the humble He shows mercy,
His compassion to the needy.

He is the Rock of all ages
He is Alpha and Omega.
When the world around us rages,
"Be still," He says. "Know that I'm God!"

THE CLEANING PROCESS

❧

Why does it hurt so much, O Lord?
And why do I feel your sharp sword
Cutting me through so deep within
While on you I'm trying to lean?

As the clay in the potter's hand,
Worked on so that each part could blend,
So is my life, my destiny
As I walk to eternity.

I feel the heat of the furnace
And the urgency of the race
As you're revealing day by day
What for us all lies on the way.

But I call on your saving grace
To find in you a hiding place
As I am cleaning my qerev*
With your word dwelling in my lev. **

Now as I'm dealing with my pain
I think of the Lamb that was slain.
His sacrifice shouldn't be in vain
As a clean life I could regain.

So grant me the strength, my Savior,
That my bitter cup I savor,
Knowing that as you overcame
I will be clean of any blame.

❦

*Hebrew word for: heart, intestines, within.
**Hebrew word for: mind, heart, the center or the middle of something.

BLOCK BY BLOCK

❧

Block by block one can build a wall,
A wall that is so thick and tall,
One no longer communicates
But embraces a selfish fate.

One can walk alone for so long,
He no longer feels he belongs
To anyone or any place
But in dreams mainly finds solace.

A kind word, a hug, or a smile
Could well be what, once in a while,
One needs his circle to brighten
And hope for tomorrow maintain.

As the ground is thirsty for rain
To produce from the little grain
That one day has been sown in it,
So one's heart needs true love to beat.

As the bee seeks from the flower
The needful pollen for honey,
So one needs from his Dulcinea
What it takes to make him stronger.

This life is not without the sun.
The heart is empty without love.
One feels lost without love
Just like a bed in an alcove.

Block by block the wall can come down.
Love and joy can richly abound.
Laughter and song can fill the air:
This would be simply nice and fair.

❧

THE BLESSED KINGDOM

❧

I know we're passing through this land
Simply as pilgrims and strangers
And I don't always understand
Some of the things we must suffer.

But there is a river of life
That brings strength and peace to the soul,
And despite all hurdles and strife,
Helps us keep our eyes on the goal.

It is in no way some mirage
To trick a lost and tired mind,
Nor a bright and blissful montage,
The simples to impress and blind.

But I know we are deeply bound
For a blessed kingdom to come
Where true love, peace, and joy abound
For those who all sins overcome.

There, I know, we'll have a mansion.
There, I know, we'll obtain a crown.
No more flesh with all its passions
To harass or drag us down.

No more sufferings and no more tears
In this blessed and glorious place.
Gone forever all pain and fears:
That's where my soul finds its solace.

THE SILENT PREACHER

Teach me to, like you, preach, o Lord,
Without the use of vain words.
Teach me how not to just well say
But to rightly walk in your ways.

As the good master and Savior,
You did not change men's behavior
With any long, blistering rants.
You simply came as a servant.

Such a dear son to the Father,
Merciful friend to the sinners,
You brought to all a ray of hope
And showed how well with life to cope.

As I follow your steps today,
I want to live my life your way.
Grant me the strength to do your will
As at your feet I learn to kneel.

A MEEK AND SWEET SPIRIT

❦

I know a meek and sweet spirit
Does not just occur overnight
As a tree does not produce fruit
Just right after one planted it.

It takes a whole combination
Of good ground, constant nurturing,
Heat, water, and the right season
To create this transformation.

Moses, the meekest man ever,
Has blessed us all with the Torah.
But to have such great character,
Went to the school of Sephora.

Joseph may have been a dreamer.
But hasn't it be for his good heart
All his life he could've been bitter
But forgiving set him apart.

Daniel and the Hebrew Children
Were deported to Babylon.
A perfect spirit they maintained
Through the furnace and lion's den.

Along the Christian walk today,
A right spirit one must display.
When facing tests and trials each day,
One should always respond Christ's way.

❧

LOVE

❧

Love!
Not a physical attraction,
A mere desire or pulsions,
An instant of pure emotion
That ends up in some deception.

Love!
Not simply gifts and nice flowers
That place one under the power
Of a possible deceiver
Who leaves one's heart reeling, bitter.

Love!
Not some type of fuzzy feeling
That keeps you constantly guessing
While one with your heart is playing
Before one's back on you turning.

Love!
So much wanted and well needed

In a sick world on its death bed!
As a dove easily frightened,
True love is hard to entertain.

For love is patient, and yet kind,
Able to bring peace to the mind.
It's not proud; it's not a boaster.
It does not dishonor others.

Love is not at all self-centered.
It is not easily angered.
It's not a collector of wrongs
That one keeps bringing as a song.

Love finds no pleasure in evil
As it flies high as an eagle;
In the truth it finds its delight
As around it all is pure light.

Love protects, and nurtures, and trusts,
Does nothing that causes disgust.
Love perseveres and never fails.
It's the wind that can make one sails.

If we could love one another,
This world would be so much better!
There won't be any need for walls
But on each other we could call.

Our children would all be safer
As to them we'd be fine teachers.
One cannot learn any better
When great model is the leader.

With love there's no need for weapons
When so well we all get along.
Love is such an excellent way
To walk in every single day!

———❧———

A NEW WORLD

❖
_____

In the candid eyes of a child,
Or in the smile of a new bride;
At the side of the elderly
Feeling so cold and so lonely
In his new place, a nursing home;
In the spirit of a woman
Rejected by her own husband,
I found a world puzzling and new
Where can reside only a few!

Some see it and say it is gold
But some others find it so cold!
This world, some have tried to explore
And bring souvenirs from its shores.
Others call it a hiding place
For some who have fallen from grace.
It's a place for meditation
Where you can hide your emotions
Yet inspire admiration!

This new world is a place for peace
If you can learn how to release
The hurtful thoughts or emotions
Caused often by life's commotions.
It can well also be deafening
If, to filter your own thinking,
You haven't yet learned to master.
It is a safe place for retreat
When with yourself you want to sit.

This new world can be paradise
Where you go at a certain price:
First, your mind needs to be rebuilt,
Set free from any shame or guilt
Thanks to God's pure and perfect word;
Then needed is a clean conscience
Deeply purged from any dead works.
For me it has made a difference
Since I found the world of silence.

SWEET FRAGRANCE

One day this race will be over.
My voice will no longer be heard.
I'll fly away just like a bird
Moving toward the bright summer.

Surely some will remember well
The moments of sweet fellowship,
The warm embrace of true friendship
That kept us like under a spell.

As I travel this path today
It is the time, it is the place
To spread around words filled with grace
That can help others find their way.

Why wouldn't I leave gentle footprints
In the hearts were I was allowed
To dwell safe in time of dark clouds
So I would not by fear just faint?

And why should not I leave behind
A melody, a sweet fragrance
To fill the void from my absence
For my loved ones, for my dear friends?

The day is coming where I'll fly.
A silent song I'll leave behind.
You might well hear it in your mind
Then you'll know I am still close by.

OTHER PUBLICATIONS BY DR. JOËL HILAIRE:

On the Other Side of the Desk (2005)

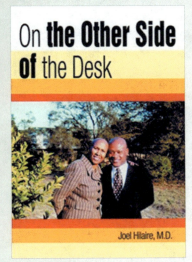

In today's world, people rush from one thing to the next and have no time to slow down and meditate. They pay no attention to their inner selves. In **On the Other Side of the Desk,** author Dr. Joël Hilaire shares one physician's efforts to trigger the desire for introspection in today's youths by helping them discover a spiritual element buried beneath the surface of their hectic lives.

When oncologist Dr. Josnel Henry, a fervent Christian, is asked to speak at the church's youth group retreat, he knows that reaching today's adolescents will be a challenge. Vowing to connect with the group without lecturing, he decides to share his true-life experiences caring for family and friends affected by cancer. His goal is to provoke soul-searching in the hope that his stories will one day spare them some of life's heartaches.

How does Dr. Henry captivate the group's attention and convey to them the valuable lessons learned through his sufferings? Does he find the right words to influence the youngsters' inner faith? Find out how adversity is turned into a stepping-stone for youth in this powerful tale of faith and personal growth.

Fantaisie de ma Jeunesse (2011)

This poetry book is mainly in French. Through the eyes of a teenager, the author presents the story of a life simply lived with modest and innocent dreams. He let transpire his quest toward the Absolute and toward Spirituality, and at the same time a desire to love and to be loved, his confidence toward friendship and his compassion before the sufferings of others.

Fantasia of my Youth, his story, your dream …

Ye Are the Body of Christ (2017)

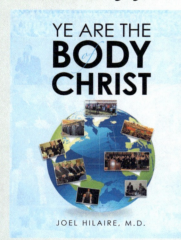

This medico-theological book presents a deep understanding of the human body to explain biblical concepts pertinent to the body of Christ. When the apostle Paul in 1 Corinthians 12:27 concludes, "Now ye are the body of Christ, and members in particular," this somehow echoes the words of King David in Psalms 139:14, "I will praise thee; for I am fearfully and wonderfully made: marvelous are thy works: and that my soul knoweth right well." Paul's comparison of the functioning of the natural body to the spiritual one gives insight into the conversations that must have taken place between "the apostle of the gospel of uncircumcision" and "the beloved physician, Luke."

In Ye Are the Body of Christ, a book tagged by some as being the first of its kind, the author skillfully uses his deep knowledge of the human body to prove biblical points concerning the Godhead, the meaning of the Crucifixion, and the biblical heart, and to demonstrate the significance of multiple diseases that have plagued humanity throughout the ages. How important is vision, naturally and spiritually speaking? How does our immune system correlate to the spiritual life? Is leprosy in the Bible the same as "modern leprosy"? What is the hidden message behind HIV/AIDS? Why do we develop cancer? Will we ever find a cure for cancer? What is the body of Christ? How should the body of Christ function? How should we care for the body of Christ?

It is amazing how the author, who is both a physician and a minister of the gospel, can effortlessly navigate through his understanding of the human body and the magnificence of the spiritual realm. Once you understand the different aspects covered in Ye Are the Body of Christ, your walk with God will never be the same.

Gemstone (2018)

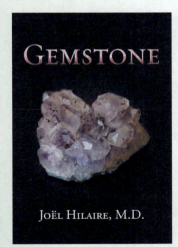

Gemstone is a cluster of poems designed to encourage, enlighten, inspire, and comfort.

Gemstone is mainly based on the author's belief and deep trust in the Word of God, especially when it comes to the power of friendship and love. Someone from his church commented, "Your poems are always great messages written artistically." Another one stated, "Your poems are very spiritual in context, and I know that is not an error." Some of the poems are the result of observation; others are the product of counseling with people facing stressful moments in their lives. Although at times a poem can transpire a gamut of human feelings and emotions when a heart is faced with the ups and downs of life, it can shine some rays of hope on us in the end. A leap of faith always transcends fear and doubt.

Gemstone's variety and composition is a delight, and its musicality is appealing to the ears. Overall, Gemstone offers good thoughts for meditation and it is an inspiration for a better tomorrow.